Messengers of Light

BY THOMAS KINKADE

MEDIA ARTS GROUP, INC.
521 Charcot Avenue
San Jose, CA 95131
1.800.366.3733

Printed in Hong Kong

Design and production by: Lucy Brown Design, Santa Barbara, California

ISBN 0-9638635-8-4

THOMAS KINKADE

Painter of Light

Thou dost keep him in perfect peace, whose mind is stayed on thee, because he trusts in thee. Trust in the Lord for ever, for the Lord God is an everlasting rock.

ISAIAH 26:3-4

I know where I've come from, I know why I'm here, I know where I'm going — and I have peace in my heart. His peace floods my heart and overwhelms my soul!

<small>BILLY GRAHAM</small>

Love the Lord your God with all your heart
and with all your soul
and with all your strength.
These commandments that I give you today
are to be upon your hearts.

DEUTERONOMY 6: 5–6

*Then they cried to the Lord in their trouble,
and he delivered them from their distress;
he made the storm be still, and the waves of
the sea were hushed. Then they were glad
because they had quiet.*

PSALM 107:28-30

Thomas
Kinkade

Show me your ways, O Lord,
teach me your paths;
guide me in your truth and teach me,
for you are God my Savior,
and my hope is in you all day long.

PSALM 25: 4–5

> *Faith is to believe what we do not see,*
> *and the reward of this faith is to see*
> *what we believe.*

ST. AUGUSTINE

The Lord is my shepherd,
I shall not be in want.
He makes me lie down in green pastures,
he leads me beside quiet waters,
he restores my soul.

PSALM 23: 1–3

I pray that out of his glorious riches he may strengthen you with power through his Spirit in your inner being, so that Christ may dwell in your hearts through faith.

EPHESIANS 3: 16–17

All that matters is to be at one with the living God to be a creature in the house of the God of Life.

DWIGHT H. LAWRENCE

In everything both great and small
We see the hand of God in all,
And every day, somewhere, someplace,
We see the likeness of His face.
For who can watch a new day's birth
Or touch the warm, life-giving earth
Or feel the softness of the breeze
Or look at skies through lacy trees
and say they've never seen His face.

AUTHOR UNKNOWN

*Love is a fruit in season
at all times, and within reach of every hand.
Anyone may gather it and no limit is set.*

MOTHER TERESA

*Summer and winter and springtime
and harvest, sun, moon, and stars in their
courses above join with all nature in
manifold witness to Thy great faithfulness,
mercy and love.*

THOMAS O. CHISHOLM

Shout for joy to the Lord, all the earth.
Worship the Lord with gladness,
come before him with joyful songs.
Know that the Lord is God.
It is he who made us, and we are his;
we are his people, the sheep of his pasture.

PSALM 100: 1–3

Joy sings in beauty that surrounds us,
Joy smiles through loved ones all around us,
Joy speaks in gentle words that guide us,
Joy smiles in feelings deep inside us.

BARBARA BURROWS

*Peace I leave with you, My peace
I give to you; not as the world gives do
I give to you. Let not your heart be
troubled, neither let it be afraid.*

JOHN 14:27

Thomas Kinkade, "The Painter of Light", is one of America's most collected artists. In the tradition of the 19th century American Luminists, Kinkade uses light to create romantic worlds that invite us in and evoke a sense of peace. Each painting radiates with the "Kinkade glow" that he attributes to "soft edges, a warm palette, and an overall sense of light."

Thomas Kinkade was born in Sacramento, California in 1958, raised in humble surroundings in the nearby town of Placerville. He attended the University of California and received formal training at Art Center College of Design in Pasadena. As a young man, Thomas Kinkade earned his living as a painter, selling his originals in galleries around California. He married his childhood sweetheart, Nanette, in 1982, and two years later they began to publish his art. In 1989 Lightpost Publishing was formed.

Thomas Kinkade is a devout Christian and credits the Lord for both the ability and the inspiration to create his paintings. His goal as an artist is to touch people of all faiths, to bring peace and joy into their lives through the images he creates.

A devoted husband and doting father to their four little girls, Kinkade always hides the letter "N" in his paintings to pay tribute to his wife Nanette, and the girls often find their names and images tucked into the corners of his works.

"As an artist I create paintings that bring to life my inspirational thoughts and feelings of love, family and faith. I hope each image in my collection acts as a messenger of hope, joy and peace to you and your family."

Index of Works